CONTENTS

ILLUSTRATIONS

All the illustrations are reproduced by kind permission of Mr. Reginald Neil, with the exception of nos. 1, 4, 5, 12, 13, 15, 16 which are from the Local Collection of Uxbridge Library.

FOREWORD

What is History? If such a question had been put to the children who attended the village school at Harefield, Middlesex, a century ago, it would have been greeted with a mixture of scorn and incredulity. From Standard II upwards everyone knew that history was about kings and queens, about wars and battles, about heroes like Clive and Wellington and villains like Richard III and whoever-it-was who caused the Black Hole of Calcutta. In short, history was about great people and great events; there were lots of names and dates to remember, but no difficult problems to solve (as in arithmetic) because Britain was always on the right side and, quite properly, nearly always on the winning side.

Those same children would have been equally incredulous to find that anyone could ever consider *them* part of "history". They were the "ungreat" — their fathers were just "the fellows who cut the hay", their mothers those who nursed the baby, fed the family and cleaned the cottage. Their lives were too ordinary, too uneventful, to interest anyone — and anyway, who was to write them down?

A hundred years on, much has changed in the writing and teaching of history. Perhaps the greatest change is that we now find the lives of our humble ancestors of engaging interest: so much has changed in the material conditions of existence in so short a time that the daily lives of our grandparents and great-grandparents now seem scarcely recognisable. In some respects their work, their dress, food and leisure pursuits seem more like those of the Middle Ages than of the late twentieth century. Yet how can the historian reconstruct those "ordinary" lives that were, to us, so extraordinary: how can he tell it "as it really was" in the visual absence of documentary evidence?

A recent approach is offered by the "oral history" method, which uses the recorded memoirs of old people to build up a picture of what life was like in past time. Obviously, oral history can extend further back than a single lifetime, and is therefore of particular value for studies of the early twentieth century, before traditional patterns of life were profoundly affected by the First World War. Not so obviously, perhaps, oral testimony of this kind needs to be handled with delicacy, discernment and the skills of the historian. He has to know the questions to be asked, of whom, and in what form, and he has to fit the answers into a pattern which draws meaningful conclusions out of individual experiences. History does not speak for itself: it has to be stood up, examined, prodded and pummelled until the facts fall out.

The following account of life and work in Harefield before 1914 is an admirable example of what the new technique, properly and professionally employed, can achieve. To those who know Harefield today it will evoke fascinating and humbling contrasts, but one does not need to know Harefield to be interested and informed by these skilfully edited reminiscences. The value of "local" history is not just parochial, for only through such detailed case studies of real people and places can we put flesh on the skeleton of our national history. Geoffrey Tyack is to be warmly congratulated on giving a voice to some of the silent multitude who, at last, are beginning to take their place in history.

JOHN BURNETT
Professor of Social History, Brunel University

PREFACE

One of the striking by-products of the transformation that England has undergone in recent years has been a burgeoning of interest in the past. Families zealously trace their origins. Local history societies and evening classes flourish. Harefield, like most of the older communities within the London Borough of Hillingdon, has experienced something of this revival of historical awareness. Its continued separation from suburban London — almost unique among the villages of old Middlesex — has perhaps made this awareness more intensely felt.

This account of Harefield before the First World War is based on a series of recordings of old inhabitants made as part of the research undertaken by a local history class which I taught in the village between 1974 and 1977. Much of the material collected by the class was published in a booklet, *Harefield at that time of Day* (1978), to which the reader is referred. I have long thought, however, that the recordings, most of them made and carefully transcribed by Mr. Reginald Neil, are of sufficient interest to merit publication in their own right, in an edited form. The earliest recorded memories begin in the 1880's, and the ensuing thirty years saw great change throughout England, not least in north-west Middlesex. But in comparison with recent years, these changes were relatively small. In some of their material conditions of life, children brought up in Harefield in the last years of Queen Victoria's reign and that of Edward VII had more in common with their Tudor and Stuart ancestors than with their grandchildren today. I have tried to explain what it was like to be brought up in Harefield, and what gave the village its special characteristics. As far as possible I have used the words of the people themselves, few of whom would have dreamt of putting their memories down in writing. I have quoted them verbatim, hoping in that way to capture the individual quality of their speech. Harefield was a largely working-class community, and the memories recorded here are those of working people.

The publication of this booklet has been made possible through the co-operation of the London Borough of Hillingdon Libraries Department, their chief librarian Mr. Colehan and the Local

Studies librarian, Miss Pearce. It could not have been written without Mr. Neil's care in making and transcribing the tape recordings, or that of those inhabitants of Harefield – some of them now dead – who agreed to be interviewed. Their names are printed at the end of the book. I am very grateful to all the former members of my class for their help, and to Professor John Burnett of Brunel University for reading and commenting on the manuscript, and for writing the Foreword. Finally, I owe a great debt of gratitude to my wife for typing the manuscript.

G. TYACK
Oxford, March 1984

Facing page: The Parish of Harefield in 1890. (O.S. map)

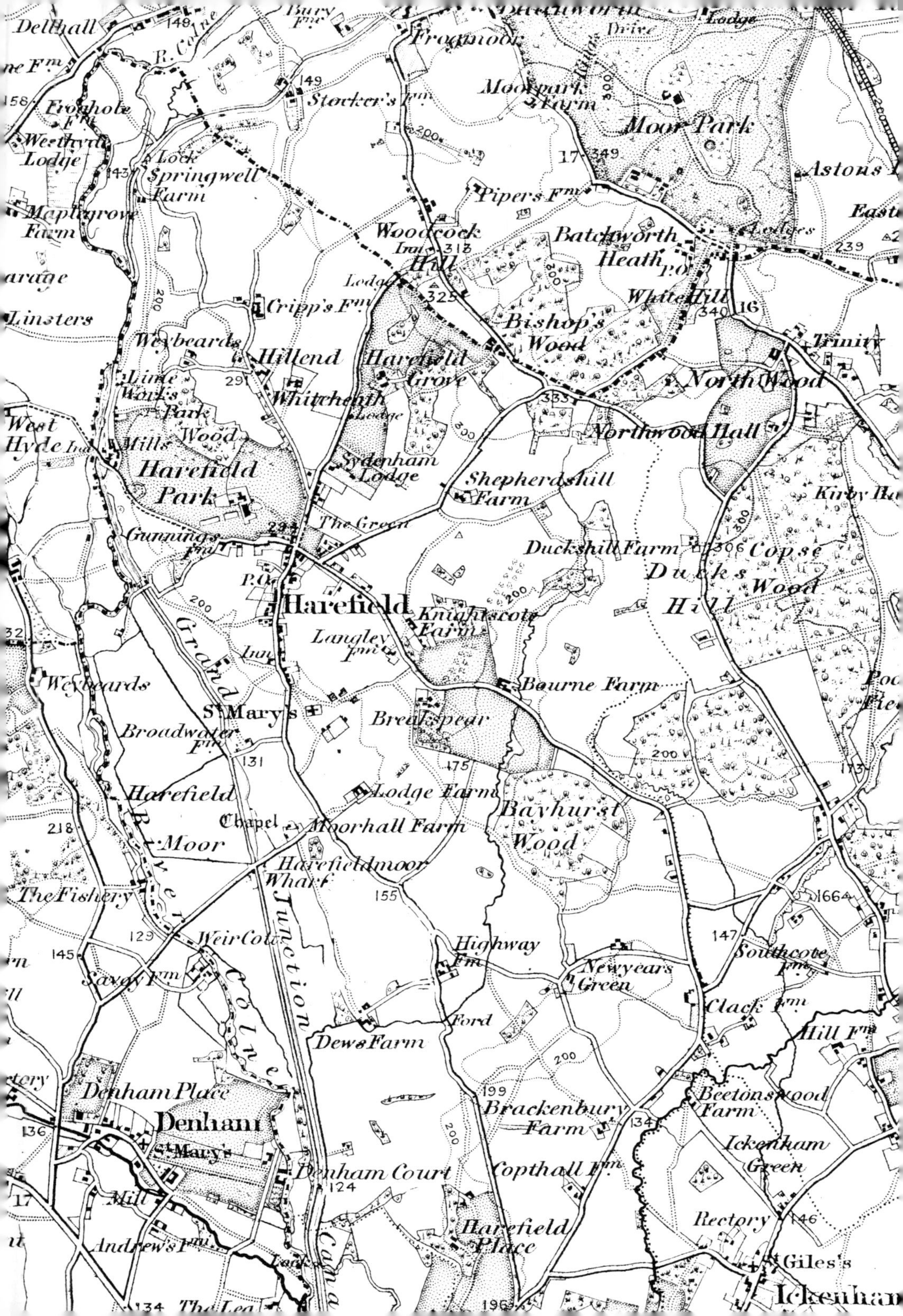
Dellhall
R. Colne
Bury Fm
Batchworth
Lodge
Frogmoor
Drive
Frogholt Fm
Westhyde Lodge
Stocker's Fm
Moorpark Farm
Moor Park
Lock
Springwell Farm
Piper's Fm
Astons
Maplegrove Farm
Woodcock Inn Hill
Batchworth Heath P.O.
Lodges
Lodge
Linsters
Cripp's Fm
White Hill
Weybeards
Hillend
Harefield Grove
Bishop's Wood
Trinity
North Wood
Lime Works
Whitcheath
Lodge
Park Wood
Northwood Hall
West Hyde
Mills
Harefield Park
Sydenham Lodge
Shepherdshill Farm
Kirby Ha
Gunnings Fm
The Green
Duckshill Farm
Copse Wood
Ducks Hill
P.O.
Harefield
Knightscote Farm
Langley Fm
Grand
Inn
Weybeards
Bourne Farm
St Mary's
Breakspear
Broadwater Fm
Harefield
Lodge Farm
Bayhurst Wood
Chapel
Moorhall Farm
River
Moor
Harefieldmoor Wharf
The Fishery
Junction
Weir Cott
Highway Fm
Southcote Fm
Savay Fm
Colne
Newyears Green
Clack Fm
Ford
Hill Fm
Dews Farm
Denham Place
Beetonswood Farm
Brackenbury Farm
Denham
St Mary's
Ickenham Green
Copthall Fm
Denham Court
Mill
Rectory
Harefield Place
Andrew's Fm
Lock
Canal
St Giles's
The Lea
Ickenham

Chapter One

The Village

Harefield has never been one of the show villages of England. A century ago it was a workaday place, set in a rolling landscape of woods, hedgerows and hayfields. The western boundary of the parish was formed by the River Colne, and parallel to it ran the Grand Union Canal. The village itself sat on a ridge overlooking the river valley. James Thorne, author of the *Handbook to the Environs of London* (1876), called it 'a flourishing and comfortable-looking country village'. He went on to say:

"Harefield is a place rich in association, and has about it much quiet sylvan beauty. It lies [overlooking] a valley, with on the one hand uplands abounding in elms and oaks and lordly houses, on the other the little river flowing gently amid broad willow-fringed meadows. The village stretches for some way along the road; has many poor and some good cottages, and the usual shops; lime and brick works; by the river a paper mill; by the canal, coal and timber wharfs."

Most Harefield people lived in or near the village street, which stretched for about half a mile along the Uxbridge-Rickmansworth road. At the southern end was the mediaeval church, with some notable monuments to local figures of the past. On an adjoining site were the ruins of the manor house, and, nearby, an attractive group of 17th-century brick almshouses. The peace of this area is now often shattered by processions of cars and lorries changing gear as they climb the hill going north, but visually at least this part of the village has changed little in the last 150 years. Further north there were rows of small plain two-storied brick cottages, interspersed with a few older timber-framed farmhouses and some larger and more recent gentlemen's houses. The front rooms of some of the houses served as shops, and there were several public houses. The focal point of the village was the green, the last remnant of the Common enclosed in 1813. From here roads branched off west down to the canal and east to Northwood and Ruislip, all of them flanked for a short distance by cottages. To the north was the hamlet of Hill End, about a mile from the main village, with some two dozen cottages, three farmhouses and a pub. At the junction of the Rickmansworth and Hill End roads there was a Baptist

Facing page: High Street, Harefield, in 1922

Chapel and a Wesleyan Chapel, and the Memorial Hall, which served as a village hall and infant school. Some new building took place in the village towards the end of the 19th century and early in the 20th century as the population rose, but the long-established pattern of settlement just described remained basically unaltered until well after the First World War.

The village was surrounded by farm land. Most of the fifteen or so farm houses were some distance away from the village centre, and approached only down narrow, rutted tracks. Nearly all the farmers were tenants of the main landowners. There were four big estates — Harefield Place, Harefield Park, Breakspears, and Harefield Grove — each centred on a country house and park, with woods carefully preserved for game, and each supporting a large establishment of indoor servants and gardeners. There were also a few smallholdings and some isolated clusters of cottages, at Moor Hall and Shepherds Hill.

The farms and great houses never monopolised employment. The Grand Junction (later Grand Union) canal was pushed through the western side of the parish close to the River Colne in the 1790s, and there was always a small population of migrant canal boatmen. Heavy goods went by boat along the canal:

"Everything went by boat then, there was no motors, everything that used to be taken to London had to come up by boat. They used to take those flints [from the chalkpits] down there, and used to bring coal back with them."

Industries developed along the canal, starting with a copper works, established during the Napoleonic Wars. This was closed down in the 1860s, but was turned into a paper factory in 1870 and finally converted in 1882 to the manufacture of asbestos. Nearby there were lime kilns, and further south a brickworks was set up in the 1860s, part of which was turned over to cement making in the 1880s.

The growth of industry coincided with a growth in Harefield's population. Throughout the south of England opportunities for agricultural employment were diminishing in the 1870s and 1880s under the pressure of cheap foreign food imports. If there was no alternative work, villagers had no option but to move away. Harefield's industries began to provide fairly stable and regular employment in the 1880s, preventing a mass exodus to the cities. The death rate was falling as sanitary reforms began to take effect. There was even a steady immigration into the village. Some came to work on the large estates, rather more to work in industry or building:

"My grandfather he came with his two brothers from Gloucester to Harefield. . .because there was no work in Gloucester,

Facing page: Church Hill, Almshouses, and the White Horse, 1921

Corner of Common, Harefield.
G. BISHOP

and they heard that there was work going on in this district in the building line, so they being bricklayers they came this way and started up in the village."

The population rose steadily, starting in the 1880s:

1851	1861	1871	1881	1891	1901	1911	1921	1931
1,520	1,561	1,579	1,503	1,866	2,008	2,402	2,812	4,140

The expansion of the population was less dramatic than in most parts of Middlesex. Harefield was not dragged from rustic isolation into rapid suburban growth. Its industries gave it diversity of employment, and its communications with London were so poor that they deterred all but the most intrepid commuters. As late as the 1920s 'every road into Harefield had a ford on it', and there were no railways close at hand. The main line of the Metropolitan Railway, opened in 1887, came no nearer than Northwood, 2½ miles away, while the Great Western's new Birmingham line, opened in 1906, passed well to the south of the village. The quickest form of transport to Northwood station at the end of the 19th century was provided by a 'fly proprietor' at the King's Arms:

"The horse-brake was the quickest. If you wanted to leave Northwood Station, he used to take you there for 18 pence. Used to have open brakes, you know. Used to be three each side and one outside. Used to take seven for 18 pence, that was the price they used to charge."

This was later replaced by a horse-bus. For those with more time, there was a daily carrier to Uxbridge and Rickmansworth. But as late as the 1920s, people going to Uxbridge still often had to walk the three or so miles to Denham station, and then catch the branch train. This relative isolation helped to give the village an inward-looking character. Despite the small influx of newcomers, Harefield remained for a long time a homogeneous working community, and not a dormitory suburb.

The failure to attract a commuting population meant that the village remained a predominantly working-class place. Most of the villagers were labourers or artisans. The artisans or craftsmen enjoyed a rather higher standard of living than the labourers, but there were fewer of them. The middle class was small. In 1881, only 21 out of 325 households — 6·5 per cent — kept servants, then an essential adjunct of middle-class status. Farmers, shopkeepers, the owners of small businesses, like the building firms and the manager of the asbestos works, were the major employers of labour. The only professional people were the clergy and the doctor, together with a few wealthy London lawyers or surgeons who bought houses in the village (like Harefield House in the village street, and Harefield Lodge, a little to the north). The top of the social ladder was occupied by the landowners. They exercised a certain amount of power, but much less

Facing page: Harefield Common (The Green) in the early 20th century

than in many smaller and more remote places. Harefield was not a 'closed village' dominated by one major landowner. Many villagers were not dependant on the land for their earnings, and had little contact with their 'natural leaders' except on social occasions and during village festivities. The landowners, like the main employers and the professional men, nevertheless sat on the parish council, formed in 1894, and took a leading part in most local activities. To this extent, Harefield society still remained a heirarchy as it always had been in the past.

Facing page: The Village of Harefield in 1916 (O.S. map)

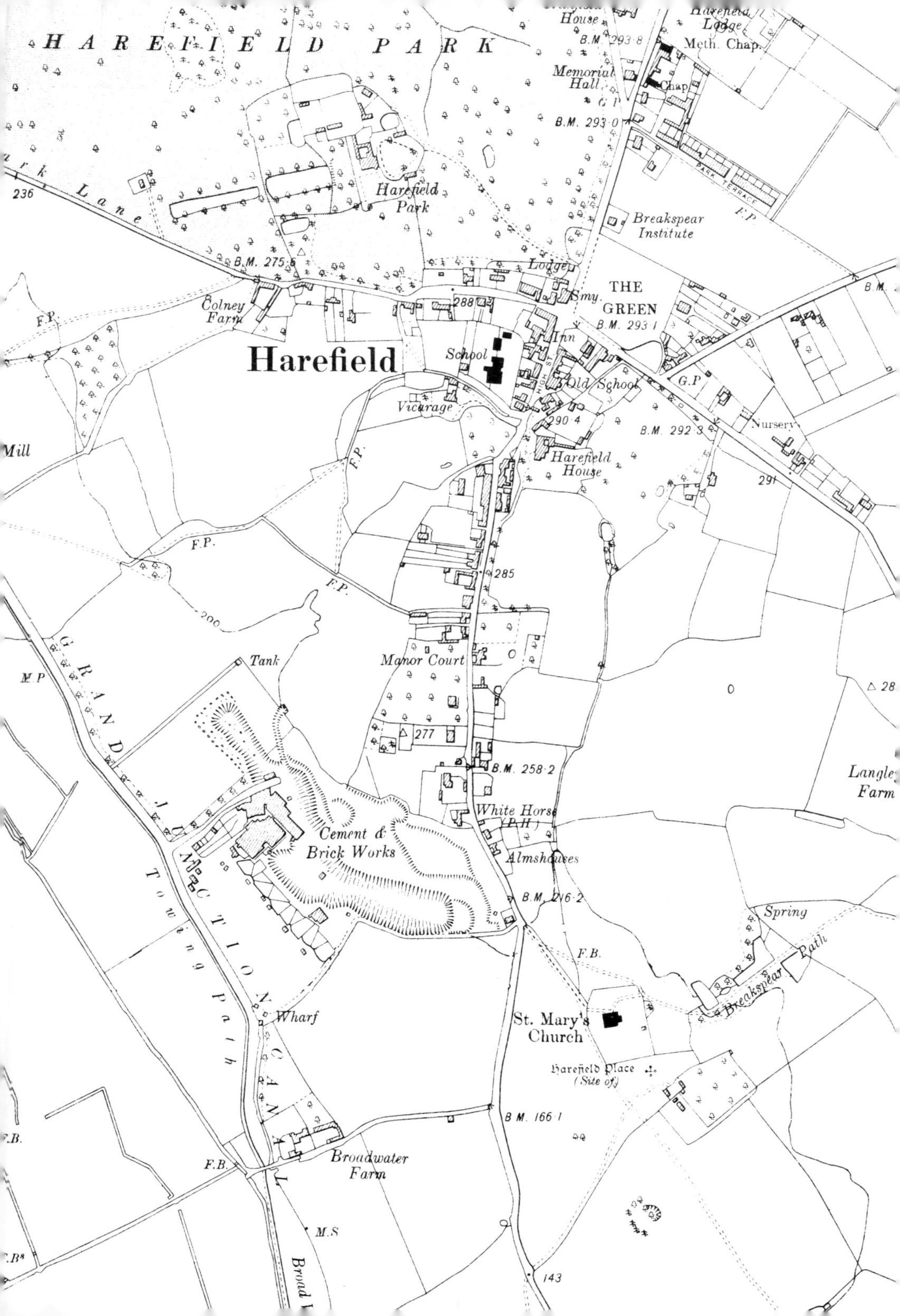
HAREFIELD PARK
Harefield
Harefield Park
House
Harefield Lodge
Meth. Chap.
B.M. 293·8
Memorial Hall
Chap.
G.P.
B.M. 293·0
Park Terrace
F.P.
Breakspear Institute
236
Park Lane
B.M. 275·6
Lodge
Colney Farm
288
Smy.
THE GREEN
B.M. 293·1
B.M.
F.P.
School
Inn
High St.
Old School
G.P.
Vicarage
290·4
B.M. 292·3
Nursery
Mill
F.P.
Harefield House
291
F.P.
285
F.P.
200
GRAND JUNCTION CANAL
Towing Path
Tank
Manor Court
M.P.
277
B.M. 258·2
Langley Farm
White Horse (P.H.)
Cement & Brick Works
Almshouses
B.M. 216·2
Spring
F.B.
Breakspear Path
Wharf
St. Mary's Church
Harefield Place (Site of)
B.M. 166·1
F.B.
F.B.
Broadwater Farm
M.S.
Broad
143

END. HAREFIELD

Chapter Two

Domestic Life and Childhood

Our earliest memories are usually of our homes. Before the First World War most Harefield people lived in small cottages, often 'two up and two down', with the upstairs rooms partitioned by curtains, and the youngest child sleeping with the mother. Some of these houses were better-built than others. Dr. Hunter, a Government medical officer, visited Harefield in 1865, and reported on the standards of accommodation:

"In Harefield *are some little old farmhouses in the hands of labourers, who enjoy about an acre of land, and are prosperous and contented. Here are old open fireplaces and appliances of two centuries ago, within a few miles of the metropolis. Nearly every house has 2 bedrooms, in which the only excessive family found was one of 6 adults with 1 child, though visits were paid at 20 houses. Rents were rising; in one row the old tenants were paying 1s 5d., while 2s 2d. was charged to newcomers. Gardens were small and the new houses very cheaply built, perhaps under £35 a house, as I could guess. Old thatches had passed away from the village, and the roofs were spouted. Isolated groups of cottages complained of being far away from the bakehouse."*

In 1881 the Uxbridge inspector of nuisances was complaining about the construction of badly-built cottages, and in 1883 he drew attention to overcrowding in Somerville's Yard, a group of six cottages which lay behind the Cricketers Inn on the western side of the village street. These cottages were eventually demolished, but there was no widespread improvement until the first council houses were built after the First World War.

The cottages of Harefield lacked most of the amenities which we now take for granted. Water was supplied by wells or pumps, several cottages sharing a pump. In one house at Hill End:

"There used to be a front room, and the old scullery at the back, and two bedrooms. No bathroom, no, a little galvanised bath, and we used to have a well, there used to be an old well, you used to have to draw your water up from the well. I used to draw it up in the bucket, keep it filled up. You could very often see a good old big frog in there, you know, jumping about."

Facing page: Hill End in 1919

There was little furniture. Sanitation was often minimal, with earth closets and poor sewage disposal. Mr. Freeman, the Uxbridge inspector of nuisances, was much occupied with the problem of polluted water supplies at the end of the 19th century; in 1884 all the wells were said to be contaminated with sewage. Despite opposition from local vested interests a new drainage system was introduced, and was described in 1887 as being 'of great benefit to the village'. Conditions, however, remained primitive even in some of the newly-built houses like Kings Cottages at Moor Hall, built in the 1890s, and known locally as the 'Old Bogs':

"[There was] one pump, between twenty houses, and there was a row of houses one side and then all the gardens and another row of houses, and of course we lived on the farthest side, so we had to go right across the gardens to get a bucket of water and more often than not when we got there the pump was broke. We used to have a water-butt outside, we used to catch all the rain water we possibly could, and when it was dry and there was no water in the butt — it was a tall one — we used to have to fill it from the pump, fill the tub up, ready for washing days."

Many cottages did not get mains water until long after the First World War. Gas did not come until then either, and electricity much later. Cottages were lit either by oil lamps or by candles. Because of the high cost of lighting, compounded by tiredness after a day of hard physical work, most people went to bed quite early, at 9.30 or 10 p.m.; the need to get up early the next day to start work further discouraged late hours, except at weekends.

Most of a family's income was spent on the three basic essentials of food, shelter and clothing. The last of these absorbed least, since clothes were cheap and long-lasting and usually handed down from one member of the family to another. *'Clothes, that was cheap, you would get a pair of boots for two bob easy'*, said one old resident. The maximum life was got out of boots and other items of clothing. One only needs to look at contemporary photographs to be reminded that for most working-class people before the First World War, clothing was drab, functional, and easily distinguishable from that of the better-off.

Expenditure on food could be kept down if it was produced at home rather than bought in the shops. Many families kept pigs:

"My father, he used to breed the pigs, and we had the bacon hanging up in the house, so we could cut our own rations. And I can remember him burning, having a big bundle of straw and burning the pigs in the old cottage, you know, to make it smoke, make the bacon. We always had two or three pigs in the sty in them days. You got the real meal, them days, barley meal, real different to what they get now, and

there's a difference in the taste of the bacon — this is not bacon what you get now, it's a lot of rubbish."

The pigs were killed at home:

"Everybody kept pigs. They used to slaughter them in the garden. Yes, just a tap between the eyes and then swing them on their back, you know, draw the knife down that way and reverse the knife and stick it in that way and let them bleed, bleed well. All the people used to have their orders, put their name down, five or six put their name down for a leg of pork. One shilling a pound, one and six in the shops."

Some people kept hens, bees, rabbits or chickens. Skimmed milk could be obtained from the farms. Vegetables were grown in cottage gardens and allotments, which took up much of the limited spare time enjoyed by labourers, especially in the summer. Children also helped in the garden:

"We didn't have much spare time. We had to work all the time. My father used to say you've got to do this and you got to do that, and we had to! I used to scour the roads round for manure, he used to make me a truck, I used to go all round the roads after the manure from horses, you see, for the gardens, because my mother never bought a potato all the year, didn't buy a piece of green at all. Every Easter my father used to say to us two or three boys, "Come on", — he was up at 5 o'clock in the morning Easter Monday — and got us some breakfast. "I want you up in that garden," he says, "to put twenty poles of potatoes in to last the year." And we did."

The importance attached to the cottage economy, based on gardens, allotments and pigs, explains the heated disputes over the 'Poors Land' in the 1890s. A party in the parish council claimed that this land, which had been given to the parish in recompense for the loss of grazing rights when the commons were enclosed in 1813, should be turned into allotments. This idea was eventually put into practice, despite some opposition. Cottage economy was also encouraged by flower shows and vegetable shows sponsored by the Horticultural Society, founded in 1885 and still flourishing.

Certain essentials of food had to be bought in the shops. Working people did most of their shopping in Harefield, only going to Uxbridge or Rickmansworth for clothes when they could afford them. For many people a visit to one of these towns was quite an event:

"Yes, we went to Uxbridge. There was an old carrier by the name of Mr. Miller, lived down Park Lane, and he had a cart and he had a big high hat he used to wear, and anything our parents wanted from Uxbridge, he'd take a list and he'd bring it back for twopence, whatever we wanted, but our biggest treat of all was to save our pocket money until we got sixpence, and to ride in this old carrier's cart to Uxbridge and back for sixpence. He'd call on the way and pick up several people's

orders and then for all their twopences bring what they wanted back. It used to be a real treat. We waited about there, there wasn't much doing in Uxbridge in those days. That was our big pleasure, that ride behind that horse and cart. He used to bring us back, and there was the ride home, which we thought was wonderful."

Food was sometimes bought from itinerant vendors:

"I can remember especially a man used to come along with rabbits, no end of beautiful rabbits, for a shilling each. He had a horse and cart. There was an old man, used to come round with china and rags, and things like that, on the cart."

Poaching flourished, not surprisingly in view of the large amount of preserved game in the parish. 'Trespass in search of game' was one of the commonest categories of cases from Harefield to come before the Uxbridge magistrates between 1878 and 1893, surpassed only by cases of assault and school truancy. Rabbits from the big estates were regularly sold in the pubs before the First World War, the poachers having taken them at night with the aid of greyhounds.

For the poorest families, diets were often insufficient, and in 1895 some villagers were said in an article in the *Middlesex Advertiser* to be in a state of 'semi-starvation'. However, according to one villager, born in 1889, 'people were strong', an observation which would seem to be borne out by the longevity of some of the men and women who are quoted here. 'Real wages' for all but the very poorest were rising at the end of the 19th century, and although this rise came to an end after about 1900, there was less grinding poverty than in the earlier years of the 19th century. Mrs. Breen (b. 1883), one of twelve children, remembered being given a hot meal each day. Stews with dumplings seem to have predominated in the diets of working class families. In some of the older cottages these meals were cooked in a way that cannot have changed much for centuries; Mr. Marsden (b. 1884) was brought up in a cottage at Shepherd's Hill with

". . .a great big old open grate with an oven on one side and a chain up the chimney with a hook on. We used to hook the pots on, hang the great big old cast iron pots on the fire. We used to have suety dumplings, used to go into the butcher's and get a pound of suet for 4d., beef suet, cut it all up in slices, and roll it all in, mix it up with flour, and make it into a good dough. We used to put bacon and onions in, parsley, spread it all over and roll it up, tie it in a cloth and put it in the soup, and boil it up. It used to last a week then. We used to cure our own bacon, never used to buy no bacon in a shop. [We would] make all the heads and all the offal into brawn, and make our own bread. Mother never bought any bread, she baked all her own bread."

Rent was another very important item of expenditure (very few working people owned their houses). Rents rose, like wages, towards the end of the 19th century, and by the First World War they seem to have ranged from 6s. to 9s. a week. Tenants of cottages in the Old Workhouse in Breakspear Road paid 6s. a week before the war, the same as the rent charged for cottages in the recently-built Waterloo Villas in the village street. The cottages belonged to a variety of people: the owners of the great estates, builders like the Colletts, and the proprietors of small businesses.

Daily life for many was dominated by the question of finding an adequate income to support a family. Most labouring families found it difficult to live on the income of the main wage-earner. Wages were low, (between about 16s. and 27s. a week for a fully-grown man in the early years of this century), and employment irregular. Agricultural and building workers were regularly thrown out of work in the winter. Sometimes unemployment was particularly high, and it never entirely went away. When people were unemployed:

"They had to get hold of what they could, what people liked to give 'em. There was relief, but you had to be qualified before you could get it, have so many children and the likes of that. You paid for your doctor, you paid for your dentist, you paid for everything didn't you, everything, from beginning to end."

Apart from poor-law relief — which in its most dreaded form meant the Hillingdon workhouse — there were only the few parochial charities and occasional help administered by the local gentry. Friendly societies enabled people to get relief on less demeaning terms; in 1885 the local court of Foresters had 349 members. Their parades were a colourful feature of the Whit Monday and 'Hospital Sunday' celebrations in the village. There were also 'clubs' like the clothing club run by the Misses Sawyer of Harefield Lodge in the 1880s, and the 'slate club' run by the Wesleyans. Another club was run by the doctor for expectant mothers, until he was forced to leave because of the inadequate income from the practice:

"They had a sort of little club, see, and those that could pay had to pay. The reason he had to go, nobody could pay him really, he couldn't afford to be there."

Financial problems were often especially pressing with large families. Village girls were advised not to get married until their early twenties, but this advice was not always heeded, and in any case, as standards of living improved (however low they might appear to us), the years of fertility for women gradually lengthened. Mrs. Kempster (b. 1888) whose sister-in-law had 22 children, remembered the village swarming with children: 'There were practically more children than adults.' Life for women was dominated by frequent and regular confinements, each of them costing 25s. for the service of one of the two village midwives.

Because income was so irregular, women and children had to earn extra money when they could. Money could also be made by taking in lodgers. When Mr. Brooker came to Harefield as a blacksmith's apprentice in 1910 he gave 12s. out of his 21s. a week to his landlord for board and lodging. Some women took in washing from the big houses. However, women with large families had little time for earning extra money. Mrs. Kempster's mother

". . .didn't have much spare time, only to wash and iron for twelve children, and cook. [She used] flat irons, there used to be an open grate and the trivet pulled out in front, and she used to put a brick on that and stand the irons in front of it so one was hot, while she was using the other."

Children had to grow up earlier than they do today, and they had fewer toys. Mrs. Breen was boarded out as a girl in the 1880s with her aunt in the lodge to Breakspear House, then rented by W. S. Gilbert, the operetta librettist:

"They were lovely people, the Gilberts were. They came to see me when I was staying with my aunt, she said to me one morning she said, "There's a gentleman and lady coming up to see you this morning, you behave yourself." So I said, "Who's that?" She said, "Sir W. S. Gilbert's coming up and Lady Gilbert." Well, this will make you laugh, they came up, so I was sitting in the kitchen, and they came in the sitting room so my aunt told them that I was there, so he said, "Oh, we must see her, we must see her, go and fetch her." So they fetched me in and he said, "Oh poor little girl," he said — I was at home with the toothache — "Have you got a dolly?" "Yes sir". "Where is it?" he said, he looked all round, so my aunt said "Go and fetch it", so I went out in the other room, and I'd got a little wicker cradle with a hood to it, and I'd got my dolly in that, so I fetched this, and I put it down at his feet, so he said "Where's the dolly?", so I picked it up, I'd only got a bit of muslin round to make the head. He picked it up and looked, and he said, "Ha ha ha ha!" He pushed two thumbs in his waistcoat, you know, and had such a laugh. He said, "That's not a dolly", so he turned to Lady Gilbert, so he said, "Couldn't you find her a better dolly than this?" so she said "Yes, I think so. When her uncle comes up to church I'll send her up a dolly." Oh, she sent me up two lovely dollies. I'd never seen a dolly like it before, because all we used to get was painted wood dollies, wood dollies, with a painted face."

Children spent a lot of their spare time out of doors:

"We used to go down to the hayfields and play in the hayfields a lot in the summer. [The boys] learnt to swim in the canal. There was a place they called Monkey Island and they used to go there and swim in the canal. I wonder they weren't drowned. They never told

Facing page: Breakspears, early 20th century

Breakshears

their parents. We used to go down there a lot when there were horse-drawn barges, and we used to get grumbled at for doing it because our parents used to think we would get tangled up with the ropes, but we still went."

The sweet-shop was a favourite resort:

"And there was an old Mrs. Bryant that lived up the yard by the butcher's shop, Beckley's yard, and in one of the little cottages she had a curtain drawn along her front door, and she had a little tiny table in front with a few sweets on and on our way to school we used to go in there and she was a great big fat old lady and she used to come and we'd say, "A farthing bootlace, please", which was licorice, and we'd have that and run out and we'd get a little way up the road, and we'd make up our mind we'd go back and have a farthing sherbet dab with the other farthing."

By the end of the 19th century all children were, at least nominally, attending school. There was a long-established National School in the village street, designed to train children in the principles of the Church of England and to teach the rudiments of literacy and numeracy. An article in the *Middlesex Advertiser* of 6 May, 1927 included an interview with Mr. Milton (b. 1845), a market gardener who operated from a cottage in the Old Workhouse:

"The scholars had to attend Sunday School and march through the village to Church to morning service, where the girls and boys bowed respectfully to the influential members of the congregation."

In 1871 an infant school was set up in the Memorial Hall by a prominent Wesleyan, Robert Barnes, a Manchester manufacturer who rented Harefield Grove. Mrs. Breen, like others of her generation, went there at the age of 3, her parents paying a fee of 2d. a week. At the age of 7 she moved to the National School in the village street:

"We learned everything. . .Reading, writing. We had little slates and pencils. Grammar was the worst, boys used to stay away from school when it was grammar. We had a sentence to parse. We had verbs, adverbs, nouns and pronouns and all that. We used to get fogged at that. [Sums] were very hard, they were sometimes, books with sums in them. Somebody bought a couple of sheep and you had to get the price of three sheep, perhaps for a flock of sheep. They were very hard. That was in the fourth standard."

The owners of the great estates 'took an interest' in the school, and there were treats:

"We used to have a mug tied round our necks and used to march up to Cox's [Harefield Place]. We had to walk all the way up

Facing page: Infants at Harefield School, 1907

Standard
VI & VII.

there with our mugs tied round our necks with a piece of tape — we always had to take mugs when we had a tea party."

The school leaving age was fourteen — there was no question of going on to secondary school — but many pupils left earlier, at twelve or thirteen, after passing a labour examination in the fourth standard. In 1908 the two Harefield schools were merged into a new council school. The type of education offered remained much the same, and discipline was strict. Mr. Lofty (b. 1907) went there just before the First World War:

"I remember I was frightened to death the first day I went [to school] because we had a schoolmaster then whose name was Mr. Blud, and he had a reputation of being a bit of a terror and I used to shake in my shoes when I first went to school."

Children from the poorer families were expected to supplement the family income. When Emily Ryder (later Mrs. Breen) won an egg-and-spoon race at school in the 1890s, the prize money went towards buying new shoes:

"I won that two or three times. I wanted a new pair of brown shoes so I run in the race and won it, so I said, "I'm going to have a pair of brown shoes!" Three shillings I won, 2s. 11d. the shoes were. They were brown ones."

Children were expected to earn money in their spare time. Mr. Statham (b. 1889) worked on the farms during his school holidays at about the turn of the century, giving his mother 1s. out of his 1s. 6d. weekly earnings, and buying bags of biscuits with the remaining 6d. Mr. Marsden sold mushrooms and acorns in Rickmansworth in the 1890s:

"Eighty years ago, if you could earn a shilling, you had to go and earn a shilling. I'd get up 5 o'clock in the morning, take a great big old basket, fill that full of mushrooms, walk to Rickmansworth — that was three mile — from the Shrubbs to Rickmansworth, go all round the greengrocer's shops and sell them. I used to get 3d. a pound for them, and I used to come back — sometimes I'd have five or six shillings worth of mushrooms in one morning, 3d. a pound. Come back, walk back to Shrubbs, give the money to my mother — she used to buy a new pair of shoes, or a suit of clothes or something out of all that money what she got. She bought all the shoes and clothes. And when the mushrooms was over, there used to be the acorns. Used to go acorning, pick up the acorns, you know. Farmers used to buy them for a shilling a bushel then. I've been out in the fields in the morning, when it's been a windy night, picked up two bushel of acorns and carried them all the way home, shot them down in the shed, and when you got about 20 or 30 bushel, you used to send to the old farmer, and he used to send a horse

Facing page: Harefield School: Standards 6 and 7, 1914

and cart to pick them up, and give you a shilling a bushel for them. He used to give them to the sheep and pigs."

Truancy was common. Mr. Statham remembered being chased over the blackberry bushes by a School Board Officer in the 1890s. There were often good economic reasons for truancy; time at school must have seemed wasted, especially when the only opportunities open to most school-leavers were various forms of labouring for boys and domestic service for girls. As one said: 'There was no such thing as going to school if you could earn a bit at that time of day'. That is not to say that some children were not encouraged to 'better themselves' by regular attendance at school. The father of one old resident, a teetotaler and non-smoker, would not let his children play truant: 'We were brought up a different way.'

When children started full-time work (which, in the late nineteenth century, could be at the age of 12) a substantial part of their wage had still to be given to their parents; Mr. Statham, for instance, kept only 2s. out of the 10s. he was getting at the age of 17 in 1906. Girls were sent into service at an early age, which cut down the demands on the family budget and also brought in some money. Sometimes, though, they had to come back home after a short time to help their mother with younger children. It was only when these younger children were themselves earning money that parents could expect to lead lives of reasonable comfort, provided they were able to remain in work. When that was impossible, the outlook was bleak indeed.

Chapter Three

Work

Many Harefield people today work outside the village, but in the 19th century it was a place where people both lived and worked. Work took up a greater proportion of people's time than it generally does today and it assumed a wide variety of forms. The types of work available played a decisive part in determining the character of the community. The main occupations are revealed in the most recent census records available to inspection, those of 1881:

Occupation of employed males in 1881

	Number	*Percentage*
Labourers	113	24·2
Agricultural labourers / Farm servants	96	20·6
Gardeners	30	6·4
Farmers and farm bailiffs	25	5·4
Brick workers	19	4·1
Carpenters	13	2·8
Boatmen (not permanently resident in Harefield)	12	2·6
Bakers	10	2·1
Publicans	10	2·1
Others	139	29·8
	446	100

Most women did not have regular employment outside the home, and of those who did the vast majority were domestic servants.

Harefield was a traditional rural community with modern industry superimposed. It was this mixture of old and new which gave the village its special character. The years between 1880 and 1914 saw an increase in industrial employment at the expense of agriculture, and in 1914 the main sources of employment were said to be in asbestos, the brick and cement works, and in gardening. Most of the employed men were unskilled labourers of one sort or another:

"There was the brickfields, and there was the factory, gardening, you know, work on the roads. . .I remember when they used to

Coppermill Hill 2

scrape the dirt off the roads, because the roads used to be very bad you know, they used to scrape all the mud off, the poor old men, and leave it in little heaps at the side."

People often changed their jobs, usually without much notice. One old resident, born in 1888, had already done four jobs by the time the First World War broke out, as an agricultural labourer, a market gardener, an asbestos worker, and finally as a labourer to the Uxbridge Rural District Council. This pattern of employment was shared by many people.

AGRICULTURE AND MARKET GARDENING

Agriculture and market gardening was the most important single source of employment in 19th-century Harefield and it remained prominent until well after the First World War. As in most of north and west Middlesex, hay was the most important crop, permanent grass taking up nearly two-thirds of the surface of the parish in 1880. There was also some market gardening and dairying. In 1899 the chief crops were said to be hay, fruit and vegetables, with some pasture.

The hay produced in Harefield was taken to London to feed its horses, and manure was brought back in return:

". . .at that time of day [before the First World War] there was all the farms — didn't do anything else only hay, and we had to take it to London, and we used to bring all this 'ere London manure back, you know, from the stables — and we spread it on all these fields, and the fields used to be white with mushrooms."

The hay was taken either by canal from the wharf by the bridge at Moor Hall, or by road. The father of Mr. Blower (b. 1888) was a 'hay jockey' in the 1890s:

". . .I used to go with him, you see, I was just a boy then. . .They used to supply the bus company and all that, because they was all run by horses, that time of day. . .Well, it would take about three hours, if you had some good horses. We used to be away at ten o'clock at night as a rule, get down the hay market at about six o'clock when the hay market opened. . .We used to stop if a pub opened, because they used to be open all night, some of these night houses."

The greatest quantities of hay were grown in the meadows near the Colne:

"All the lower meadows of Harefield, which is by the Halfway House right along as far as Denham Lock, and going right along as far as Rickmansworth the other way, were flooded early in March and produced three crops of hay in the year instead of one, because of the flooding. This made the grass grow a lot quicker and it was at least five

Facing page: Coppermill Hill (now Park Lane) in 1911

weeks earlier than in any other part of Harefield, let alone the rest of Middlesex."

Technological changes did not greatly affect Harefield farms until the first appearance of tractors. As late as the 1930s:

"There were no modern fertilisers, and in the winter, dung was regularly spread on the fields to prepare for the next crops. Bourne Farm had six horses, Turners Farm had I think it was twenty horses, that was the largest farm in Harefield in actual fact. There we had 10 pairs of horses, because you used horses in pairs, because all the machinery at that particular time wasn't particularly heavy, but the ground was waterlogged to get over, so therefore you had to have two horses to do one horse's job in actual fact. . .And there was something that was more human about life then than it is today. You know if you drove a pair of horses from 8 o'clock in the morning until 12, you know they'd had enough. If they'd been pulling a plough for that particular day, they were looking towards the gate to get back to have a rest."

Dairying became increasingly important in the 20th century . The cattle were driven to market on foot. Mr. Statham remembered doing this job as a boy before the First World War:

"I used to go to Wendover to meet cattle coming from Aylesbury, that was about half way you know, then drive them all the way from Wendover to Hill End. I went by train from Rickmansworth to Wendover. . . I used to meet another driver then. He used to go back by train, that way, to Reading, and I used to come back, walk 'em home. . . They would be mostly bullocks and sometimes you might have about a dozen bullocks, or you might have about fifty sheep. . . Oh, I thought there was nothing like it, you know. I used to wear some boots out!"

Between the wars large herds were kept in the 'lower meadows' near the Colne:

"They used to support something like 700 cattle down there throughout the summer and right up until about October time, until as I say it got so wet that you would start losing them — you would literally lose them. . . I can remember in the winter time when it has been really heavy rain, going down there in the morning to feed them and finding 5 or 6 of them with only their heads and horns just sticking out of the ditches you know. This is what it was like."

Farm workers began work at an early age. Mr. Statham began helping out on farms in the school holidays in the 1890s:

"I used to generally work on the farm, you know, do odd jobs on the farm. I remember working for about I think nearly five weeks, and I had eighteen pence after the five weeks."

For his first full-time job he got 5s. a week for an eleven-hour day, rising to 10s. at the age of 12, by which time he 'felt quite rich.'

Boys who had just left school were put on to weeding or bird-scaring, like Mr. Blower at Knightscote Farm in about 1900:

"Bird scaring, out in the fields for the farmers, keep the birds off the corn when it had been fresh sown you know. Well, you had to walk about the fields when they came over. . . Several [boys] used to do the job. We might get a couple of bob at the end of the week perhaps. You had to be there Sundays and all. You had to be there in the morning as soon as it got light, to keep birds off."

Some children followed their fathers into agricultural work. Mr. Marshall (b. 1898), whose father was cowman on the Breakspear estate, began his working life by milking cows for 6s. a week, after which he became third gamekeeper at 10s.

Farm work was irregular. Farms which specialised in hay farming — the majority before the First World War — needed only a skeleton year-round work force, although large numbers of part-timers, both men and women, were employed each July during the harvest. At Broadwater Farm, according to an account book now in the G.L.C. Record Office, the total wage bill did not rise above £3 for the first five months of 1904, but reached £9-6s.-0d. in the third week of June, and £20-9s.-6d. in the first week of July, falling to the original level of between £2 and £3 by the first week of August, where it remained. There was a lot of seasonal unemployment, when agricultural workers had to find work in the local factory, brickworks or cement works, or to 'tramp' in search of work, like Mr. Lofty's father:

"I can remember him telling me about walking to Yorkshire to get work, picking up jobs on his way there and doing a harvest there, and then walking all the way back to Harefield."

Wages were low. In the 1880s, fifteen or sixteen shillings a week was a common wage for a grown man, rising a little at the end of the century. Regular employees like carters were sometimes offered a rent-free cottage in addition. There was also a bonus at harvest time:

"All the farm labourers had that, used to have sixteen bob a week and a house. . .never got no more, nor no less. In the summer, like, when they was haymaking and harvesting — when they was done, they used to have a Harvest Home. . .y'know, as much beer, and as much as they could eat — and a sing-song. . .then they used to get £5. . .that was £5 for all the overtime they done. [It] used to be 16s. a week, and £5 at Michaelmas."

Market gardening, like dairying, expanded in importance as London's population grew and its tentacles spread out into north-west Middlesex. Most of the gardens were quite small, like that run from a cottage in the Old Workhouse by James Milton. There was a larger market garden at Harefield Grove in the 1880s and 1890s, but its owner, Mr. G. Webster, went bankrupt in 1896. The vegetables from

Harefield's market gardens were taken both to London and, from the end of the 19th century, to nearby suburban communities like Northwood and Pinner. Mr. Marsden worked, like his father, at Harefield Grove in the 1890s:

"My father worked at Harefield Grove for sixteen year — he was a gardener — he used to look after the lawn, and done all the flower beds, and rose beds, and got to look after the lawn. Him and a boy, he used to have an old pony to do the mowing, and him and the boy, they used to look after all the flower beds. . . All I used to do was water all the flowers, cucumbers, tomatoes, that sort of thing, that's all I done. I'd 6s. a week, and I used to work from 6 o'clock in the morning till 6 o'clock at night. . . I used to have half an hour for breakfast, an hour for dinner — ten hours and a half a day for six bob a week."

There were also orchards in the village, like Mr. Collett's in Church Hill, where Mr. Harman (b. 1896) got his first job after passing the labour examination:

"Well my first job, when I was 13 you see, I left school in the morning. The teacher said, "Well, there's only two passed", a girl and me. So I rushed home and told me mother, "I've finished school, shan't go back any more, Ha! Ha!" So Mr. Collett he had a row of houses, you know, what we used to call Casey Court, and in that piece of ground he had some trees, apple trees, and he kept looking after them, you see. . . I went out after I had had my dinner and he was there, you see, in this orchard, and he said, "Who are you?" (He knew who I was). He said, "How is it you're not at school?" I said, "I've left school." "Left school?" he said. I replied, "Yes". He said, "Do you want a job?" I said, "Yes". "All right", he says, because my grandfather used to work for him. "Well, you go and tell your granfer", he said, "Come down with him at 6 in the morning", he says, "tomorrow morning and I'll give you 5 shillings a week". . . He had a big orchard, and what I did, he had three or four Welsh ponies and he used to sell this fruit and I got a Welsh pony with a covered van, I used to load. I used to catch my horse up Vernon Drive, that was his field, Vernon Drive, catch my horse up there in the morning at six o'clock, bring it down, and put it in the van and go and load up my van with fruit and off I'd go to Northwood, Pinner, and Harrow and selling this 'ere fruit at fourteen years of age."

SERVANTS AND ESTATE WORKERS

Domestic service was the biggest source of employment for women for many years. The owners of the largest houses kept big indoor staffs. In 1881, W. F. Vernon of Harefield Park (now part of the Harefield Hospital) employed 16 people, most of them women: a butler, two footmen, a coachman, a cook-housekeeper, three ladies' maids, a

Facing page: Captain Tarleton's car and chauffeur outside Breakspears, 1921

BREAKSPEARS.

FIRE.

On the Fire Bell being rung, Every outside man is to go to the Fire Engine House at once, and as quickly as possible.

The 1st two men who arrive are to pull out the Manual Engine, (and if at night to light the lamps), without waiting for orders.

If the fire is at the House itself, the Manual Engine is then to be placed as soon as there are enough men to man it, on the Drying Ground, and connect with the tank at once, and three lengths of Delivery Hose to be immediately put on.

The first man of the Steam Engine's crew is to commence to raise steam at once and when ready blow a long blast on the whistle.

THE FOLLOWING ARE THE SPECIAL DUTIES FOR EVERYONE.

NAME.	PLACE.	DUTIES.
MAID SERVANTS And all persons not mentioned below	Business Room	All the Maid Servants are to assemble in the Business Room and wait for orders, except the Lady's Maid and Nurse, who have special instructions. If at night the Housekeeper is especially responsible that all the maids are there, and that the Nurse is acquainted with the alarm. Each upper servant is to see that her under servants are present.
BUTLER	At Fire	To lock plate room, and secure cellar keys, and lock lamp room door, see that Mr. Tarleton is sent for if away, then attend at the fire, having seen that visitors and their servants are called.
FOOTMEN	No. 3 Pump	To work No. 3 pump under directions of the Butler.
HEAD GARDENER	At Steam Fire Engine	To see that the Engines are properly connected, and give the necessary orders for the number of lengths of hose, when everything is ready bring the hose to the fire.
DAIRY KEEPER & MAN	Manual Engine	See to the animals, if necessary, then to Manual Engine.
COACHMAN & GROOMS	Manual Engine	See to the horses, if required, then go to Manual Engine to pump.
KEEPER AND UNDER KEEPERS	Manual Engine	Attend to the pumpers and work with Manual Engine.
DUTY FOREMAN	Manual Engine	To work with the Manual Engine, and be ready to go to the Telegraph Office and Police Station.
OFF DUTY FOREMAN	Manual Engine	To work with the Manual Engine.
1st UNDER GARDENER	Steam Fire Engine	To work with the Steam Fire Engine.
2nd "	Steam Fire Engine	1st fetch ladder and place it under the Nursery Window, then Steam Engine.
OTHERS	Engines	To work with the Engines.
BOYS	With Mr. Tarleton	Get whistle and ambulance bag, and attend with Mr. Tarleton.
CARPENTER	Ditto	Attend with Mr. Tarleton, and as required to be ready with Tools.
UNDER CARPENTER	Steam Fire Engine	Help with ladders, then go to Steam Fire Engine.
STABLE HELPERS	Stable Pump	Work Stable Pump, if not required, then Manual Engine.
UPPER LODGE KEEPER	Manual Engine	To work with Manual Engine.
BAILIFF		Send to House at once to enquire if Farm hands are wanted; if at night come to House, first taking measures to arouse all farm hands.

The above duties apply more especially to the case of Fire at the House.

Pumping is to commence at the sound of the whistle. It is to cease on the whistle sounding again.

If the Lamps are used one is to remain at each Engine and the other used along the hose if required, but always to be returned to the Engine it belongs to.

All the men are to wear their caps whether it is practice or not.

The Steam Fire Engine's Crew consists of Head Gardener, Carpenter and Under Carpenter, and 2 under Gardeners.

As soon as steam is up, at the sound of the long blast the men will cease pumping, disconnect the Manual and connect the Steam Engine. Then all except the Steam Engine's Crew will assemble where directed to save furniture, &c. If no directions have been given they will stand clear and wait for orders.

GENERAL REMARKS.

Whenever the Bell is rung it is always to be assumed that the House is on Fire.

The above orders apply to the Alarm of Fire, and as everything depends on promptitude, everyone is to take up their station as quickly as possible, but remembering that hurry is of no use if their duties are not carefully attended to.

The small Fire Pumps in the House and Stables are intended to be used at once on the outbreak of Fire, and if promptly brought and put in action, may be the means of Stopping a fire before it has time to spread. The Maid Servants as a general rule are to be prepared to work No. 1 and No. 2 pumps.

If the Fire is away from the house, and the Engine has to be driven, no more than 3 men besides the driver are to go on it, and they are always to get off on going up anything like a steep hill.

In the Absence of Mr. Tarleton, the Butler is to take charge of the arrangements if the Fire is in the House; the Coachman if it is in the Stables; the Head Gardener if it is anywhere else. In the absence of the Family the Head Gardener is to take complete charge of all arrangements, and if he is away the Carpenter is to take his place

nurse, two laundry maids, three housemaids and two kitchen maids. The great houses were run on heirarchical lines. At Breakspears, as late as the 1920s:

"There was a set way of life for the staff. The housekeeper, butler, lady's maid and head housemaid all ate in the servants' dining hall for the meat course, but retired to the housekeeper's room for the pudding. Tea was taken in there too, with a maid to lay and clear away."

Most of the servant-keeping households were much more modest than this. The vicar had three servants, a nurse, a housemaid and a cook in 1881, and the farmers and small manufacturers or businessmen had to rest content with only one or two, a 'cook general', and sometimes a housemaid.

Many village girls had to go out of the village for their first jobs in service. Emily Breen first came into contact with her social 'superiors' when she was living with her aunt in the entrance lodge to Breakspears:

"[My aunt] used to open the gate for the carriage, and when she wasn't there I had to go and do it. "Now", she used to say, "You'll be sure and curtsey when they go along." I said, "All right, Aunt, I will", and I used to have to curtsey."

Her first full-time job, though, was obtained through the owner of Harefield Lodge, whose sister married the vicar of Chingford in Essex:

"My mother got me a little place in service, and I went down to Chingford, and I lived with the vicar down there, in the vicarage. It was beautiful."

The wage was 2s. 6d. a week. Servants had to buy their own clothes:

"No, we had to find it all. There were cotton dresses and black dresses and house shoes and everything, caps and aprons, all to buy. I was very happy down there."

Emily Breen returned to help her mother look after the younger children, and was then employed by the Harefield doctor, Dr. Little, as cook-housekeeper at Hill House (now demolished). The other servants were a housemaid, and a coachman whom she eventually married. Her day began at 6 a.m. and she had half a day a week off, and every other Sunday.

Many Harefield girls went into service in London. Mrs. Green (b. 1896) started her career at the age of 13, working part-time for two ladies in Harefield, finally taking a job in Hampstead as a parlourmaid just before the War. Here she started at 7 a.m., and sometimes worked 14 hours a day. The duties were onerous: 'If you lived in you were always on duty. We used to get frightfully tired'. Pay was low, and there was only one day off each month, in which she came home to

Facing page: Fire Regulations from Breakspears at the turn of the century

Harefield on the Metropolitan line to Northwood, and had to go back the same evening. But apart from the shops, which provided the most desirable type of work, there were no other jobs for girls in or around Harefield until the First World War. Then the expansion of the asbestos works gave the opportunity for more and better-paid employment, albeit under conditions of mass-production.

The great estates had large outdoor staffs of gardeners, gamekeepers, and maintenance men. There were seven gamekeepers in Harefield in 1881. Breakspears was run on a particularly grand scale. From the late 1880s it was the home of Captain Tarleton, an equerry to the Duke of Albany, and his wife, who was related to the Duke of Newcastle:

"He used to keep — oh — a coachman, two grooms, four or five horses, old Tarleton did. He got six servants, six gardeners, butler, footman, and there used to be one bloke, he used to be in the house, cleaning all the lamps, and he had to fill them up and look after the lamps, that's all he used to do. He had an estate carpenter, Mr. Burt, and old Bull was the head gardener. Old Stone — he was head coachman. He had three keepers. They all got the sack because they got drunk one day. They was supposed to be working, and somebody went and got them all out of the pub, drunk. They all got the sack, all three of them."

There was also a chauffeur and a carpenter, who looked after the fire engine, the only one in the village.

The life of Breakspears under the Tarleton regime revolved to a large extent around shooting, and the estate's proximity to London made it a popular venue for shooting parties. In the words of one of the former gamekeepers:

"When the estate was running they used to shoot 600 pheasants in one day, and I used to go and carry Captain Tarleton's gun and cartridges, and rain-coat and that sort of thing. And he used to usually have eight guns, plus himself, and they used to start at 9 in the morning, and shoot pheasants all day and then at 4 o'clock in the afternoon they used to go duck-shooting and that lasted a couple of hours. And they've had as many as 200 duck in one afternoon. There was always 8 guns and Captain Tarleton had a horn, which he used to signal the game-keeper, and my job was to go round and put about twenty boys out, what they call stop-gap, early in the morning. They used to get one shilling a day and a pork dinner you know, a beef and pork dinner and a bottle of lemonade each, you see. And then as the shoot went on you picked them all up and then they followed you so that at night time you'd got the Whole consignment with you."

Gamekeepers spent much of their time guarding against poachers:

"Oh yes, it was terrible, but we always used to get the signal

Facing page: Captain Tarleton (Middlesex Biographical and Pictorial, *1907)*

from other estates. Lord Ebury, the Park, where the present hospital is you see, and the Grove, they had game-keepers, they all had gamekeepers. Even out-lying, Swakeleys at Ruislip, and if these poachers were moving around you got the signal that they would be in your area perhaps at that time, you prepared for them. You used to have to bush all your woods, what you done was to put bushes all along, so the 100 yards net where they run out got tangled up, and, you see, they used to do it at night time, they used to travel round in horse and van in those days, pony and trap and greyhounds and with this 100 yards nets, you see, slide along the wood and everything of course outside it run back into the wood."

The job was not without its compensations. A gamekeeper had a tied house on the estate, and there were also tips:

"Yes, they were a marvellous family really. You didn't come in touch with them much, only occasionally you know, not every day, on shooting days. But he used to give me a brace of pheasant, or a duck and a pheasant every year, plus your Christmas bonus, a joint of beef or money. Because you had tips. You had tips at every shoot you see. The tips in those days was a golden sovereign or a half a golden sovereign."

SHOPS AND SMALL BUSINESSES

Like other large villages, Harefield was much more self-sufficient than it is today. Many goods were made or processed in the village. Bakers made their own bread, and there was a slaughter-house behind the butcher's shop which shared premises with the King's Head inn:

"They killed pigs there, we used to help there, pull the bullock through on a ring through a chain, put his head on a block and Old Smacker, they called him, he'd used to pole-axe it. That was done in the slaughter house, every Monday night, and he'd wait for the kids to give him a pull out, he'd only have two or three of you, give a good pull, pole-axe it, then they used to kill the pigs and sheep and all. Mrs. Bray at the Nelson used to have the chitterlings, then she'd sell them Thursdays, take your basin, sixpence a pound."

At the end of the 19th century there was a timber firm, a coal merchant's, a blacksmith's shop, a wheelwright's, a saddle-maker, a brewery and two building firms. Some people combined this sort of work with farming. Ratcliff's brewery in Park Lane employed five people in 1881, the brewer doubling up as a maltster and farmer of 24 acres. Mrs. Breen could still remember the malthouse functioning before its closure at the end of the 19th century:

"It was just a brickwork with two windows, one here and one there and they were wooden and they kept them closed, but once a week they used to open them and we used to sit up when we came out of

school, to watch, on the sill to see what happened. There was a big pool inside with brickwork round it, you know a big round one and all this malt, it used to come down a shute from above, they used to take it in sacks, bags, and then they sent it, it all used to come down in the pool, they used to soak it in there, then it used to go to the Brewery."

There were several one-man or family enterprises, like the shoemaker's shop run by Mrs. Gough's father:

"I'll tell you how long it took him to put a pair of soles on a pair of boots, he cut them out all ready and he'd go round one in five minutes. He used to have these hides, you know, about nine foot long by four, five foot wide. He used to do it all himself. Sometimes he would start at 7 o'clock in the morning and knock off for a bit of dinner. He'd go on and perhaps he go in tea-time for a cup of tea, then he would carry on until 8 o'clock at night, have a wash, then out. Down to the White Horse."

Other businesses employed a few assistants. Mr. Brooker was apprenticed as a blacksmith's assistant. He got 21s. a week for an 11½ hour day, but later left because he was refused a pay rise, and went to work as blacksmith at the brickfields. Here the hours were even longer:

"Well [I worked] all hours, when you got there and there was a breakdown you didn't stop until it was finished. [You'd] never know what time you was going to get away from there."

Successful entrepreneurship could bring substantial rewards, at least by local standards. Another blacksmith, Charles Filkins, branched out into building and undertaking at the end of the 19th century, and the undertaking business continued into the First World War, when it was kept busy by the presence of the hospital for Australian soldiers at Harefield Park:

"Old Charlie Filkins used to be the undertaker. He used to bury them for 50 bob. 50 shillings funeral it used to be, and old Frank Carter — he was the carpenter — used to make the coffins. He used to have a three-wheel truck, used to take the coffins from there, put the coffin on, take them down to the churchyard. There weren't no hearses — not at that time of day. They pulled an old long truck with three wheels, you know — a man was in front. Yes, there was no such thing as a hearse, never had enough money to pay for a bloody hearse. You'd got to be a millionaire if you had a hearse. I buried, I don't know, must be a hundred Australians. I used to be there at nights, and Saturdays, to dig the graves for them. Everybody was in the army then, they couldn't get nobody to dig graves and that. You'd be at the pub, and say so-and-so died, "Who'll go and dig his grave?" Well, you used to go out of the pub, and dig a grave for him at nights."

The Filkins family later took over an ironmonger's shop and ran a bus and taxi firm.

There were a few small retail shops. Opening hours were elastic, and working hours long. Mrs. Challis, the hairdresser, got most of her customers after the pubs closed on Saturday nights. According to one former customer:

"I must have been about 16 I should think [in about 1900]. It used to be 2d. a haircut, 1d. a shave then, that's as much as she used to charge. She used to keep open till 10 or 11 o'clock at night at that. She used to stop while the pubs turned out, then they used to go and have a shave after the pubs turned out, she used to be up until 12 o'clock at night, shaving people, only Saturday, only used to shave once a week, then, they couldn't afford no more than a penny."

Mrs. Westbrook worked as a girl in Reed's draper's shop, one of the more modern retail establishments which began to appear in the village after the turn of the century. She started at 8 a.m. and worked until 9 p.m. six days a week, with a half-hour dinner break. Her wage was about 12s. a week. On Saturdays the shop stayed open until 10 p.m.:

"There was two special customers, an old Mrs. Birch and an old Mrs. Cutts and I used to dread seeing them come in, because they'd leave their shopping till half past 9 on Saturday night, and then they used to come to my shop, and they'd either want a pair of pants or a pair of trousers for their husbands, and perhaps I'd have to pull out bundles and bundles before they made their choice, and of course it was after 10 o'clock before I could close the shop."

Some of the shops did much of their business by delivery, and much of a shop assistant's time was taken up with making up orders for people who lived in outlying parts of the parish. Delivery was by horse and cart:

"My grandfather was a greengrocer in Harefield, and he also worked at the cement works, and then made his living at greengrocery. Well my father used to work for him and go to Covent Garden to pick up the greengroceries and vegetables to bring back to Harefield, and they used to sell them that evening. I remember they used to do the round in the evening, by horse and cart. It was all done by horse and cart. Nearly everything in Harefield was done by horse and cart."

BUILDING AND BRICK-MAKING

Harefield's population was growing, and with it the demand for houses. Two families did particularly well out of this demand. Charles Brown, who first appeared as a small builder in the mid 19th century, also farmed at Conduit and Whiteheath farms in the 1880s and '90s, and in 1884 had 70 employees and apprentices. His sons set themselves up as small farmers. His great rivals were the Colletts, who built several of the cottages in the village, and rented them out; in the words of one informant, they 'owned Harefield' in the years just before the First World War. They built a large house (Cumberland House, now the Vicarage) in the High Street, and became substantial local figures. Mr. Harman's uncles worked for them:

"My father's brothers were two brick-layers and they built the Vicarage as it is now, a lovely brick built building and [the Colletts] gradually got on, and borrowed money, and then they bought nearly all the old houses up in Harefield."

In the 1920s Harefield was still famous for its good brick-layers. According to one of them, a bricklayer underwent five years' apprenticeship, working a twelve-hour day. At the end of the First World War a boy could earn 12s. a week.

An important by-product of the building boom in late 19th-century Middlesex was the opening-up of brickfields. The Harefield brickfields flourished up to the First World War, drawing people from the surrounding villages. Mr. Harman got a job there in 1913, when he was 17, and joined his father who already worked there:

"In the brickfields there was five places where they made bricks, you see, five places, and in this brickfield in one stall, there was about three men and a lad and two bigger ones. And they worked from 6 in the morning to 6 at night, making bricks. My father, he was really the quickest one there, you know, it's true, and he used to make 800 an hour one at a time."

The industry was organised in a way which put a great deal of responsibility on to the individual brick maker, and there was a great incentive, fostered by piece-work rates, to work fast. It was possible for a man to make about 27s. a week in the brickfields at the time of the First World War, but this was only by enlisting the help of members of his family:

"[My father] used to do this piece-work, mind, and my brothers and I used to have to go down after we left school, after we come out of school at nights, and rake his sand over ready for the next day's working, you know. They used all hand-made sand-faced bricks, and we used to go down there and rake his sand over for the next day, so that he'd got plenty of sand for the next day so that he didn't have to do it himself in the morning. Every lad from the family had to do that when the people were working in the brick works."

Hours were long and there were few holidays (brick makers worked all day Saturday). Work began very early in the morning:

"We used to have an old dog that [my father] used to take to work with him, an old black retriever dog, and he used to send her up at breakfast time for his breakfast. Mother would cook his breakfast, put it

Overleaf page 48: Employees at the Asbestos Works, 1891
page 49: Bell's Asbestos Works in 1913

1891
DEPARTMENT
L.D

BELL'S UNITED ASBESTOS COMPANY LTD.

AA
2221

in a basket, give it to the dog, and away she'd go and take his breakfast down to where he was working in the brickyard."

Bricks were either taken by boat along the canal to London, or by road to nearby places where they were needed for building:

"The local bricks which were sold from the brickfields was put into carts with just 500 bricks, and what they had years ago down this brickfield was half a dozen of these large horses, dray horses from London and they used to pull these bricks to Northwood, 500 a time, twice a day, that was their day's work."

CEMENT AND ASBESTOS MANUFACTURE

Cement and asbestos production provided the bulk of Harefield's industrial employment at the beginning of the century. The cement works were adjacent to the brick works, and soon employed many more people. Cement manufacture requires both chalk and clay, and these materials had first to be extracted from the hillside:

"[They] used to make all the cement and bricks with the clay and chalk. Used to have great big washmills, used to wash the chalk and cement and that, chalk and clay. Used to keep going round with drags, and making all of it into a slurry, and then that used to go into kilns, and they used to burn it with cement, and they used to make bricks with it."

The cement was carried down to the barges on the canal. Work was organised in 8-hour shifts, with a continuous 18-hour shift every third weekend. One weekend in three was allowed off, but otherwise men worked for seven days a week, and there were no regular holidays. Mr. Blower's father looked after the horses and the works:

"They had 9 or 10 horses, you see, they got no motors, that was before motors came on the road. He used to get down there early in the morning, a couple of hours before, feed 'em and clean 'em, and the drivers just had to come and take them out. He'd get down the stables at about 4 o'clock in the morning. Well, sometimes he started before then, all depends on how he felt. He said he never finished until 7.30 or 8 o'clock at night. He worked every day, seven days a week, not like these days!"

Much of the cement was taken by barge to the asbestos works, and when they closed down, cement production ceased too.

The asbestos factory was the most highly organised industrial enterprise in Harefield from 1882, when the United Asbestos Company took a lease of Harefield Mill. It eventually became the biggest employer, drawing people not only from the village but also from surrounding places like Denham, West Hyde and Uxbridge. Between two hundred and three hundred people were employed in the factory

Facing page: An Incident near the Asbestos Works, 1912

in the 1890s, but production seems to have been in decline before the outbreak of war; one Harefield inhabitant recalled leaving the firm in about 1913 because he did not agree with a strike which had been called over a proposal to run down production. Asbestos was made out of cement from the cement works with fibre brought down the canal from Brentford. The factory was divided into sections, according to the materials manufactured. By the end of the First World War the firm was making brake linings, fire containers, and cladding for pipes. Many of the men were involved in the manufacture of Poilite sheeting, which was used among other things as cladding for houses (a "Poilite house" was advertised in 1919). Others were in the 'heavy gang', loading and unloading barges, and transporting coal for the boilers. As in the cement works, work was done in shifts, and in the early days before the war discipline seems to have been rather lax. According to one account: 'We used to have a holiday when we thought we would, when we got tired.'

The coming of war greatly increased the demand for asbestos, and the workforce was greatly expanded, only to fall victim to the Depression in 1929. There were about two thousand employees in the early 1920s, and a number of people, especially women, came from far afield and settled in the village. The firm apparently 'believed in Unions', and the men joined the National Union of General Workers. There was a Works Committee consisting of management and men. There were, however, no paid holidays, and working hours lasted from 8 a.m. till 5.45 p.m., with an hour for lunch. A boy starting work was paid 4d. an hour, rising after completing apprenticeship to £4 a week. The asbestos works were an outpost of modern industrialism in what was still a rural village, and they paved the way to the transformation of Harefield's character which began between the wars.

Chapter Four

The Community

Working people had less free time in the late 19th century and early 20th century than they do today. There were few holidays: 'We weren't allowed to have any holidays, that time of day', said Mr. Blower. 'No holidays except for the usual Easter and Christmas'.

Crowded and often insanitary conditions at home drew people outside for their leisure activities. Men went to the pubs or worked in the summer on gardens or allotments, while children played outside in the fields, by the canal, or on the cement works:

'We did like our fathers did, work on the allotment. We used to have to go to church every Sunday morning. We used to generally go out for walks Sunday evenings. We had to make our own enjoyment then, that time of day, the best we could."

Like most villages before the First World War, Harefield was a closely-knit place. Most people worked in the village, and they spent most of their spare time there too. Before her marriage in 1919, Mrs. Kempster had not been further from her home than Uxbridge. The Harefield shops provided for most of the everyday needs of working people. Only the rich had their own means of transport, and public transport was poor. People walked more often, and for greater distances than they do today; even when bicycles began to appear at the end of the 19th century, few people could afford them.

Uxbridge, a market town with large shops and chain stores (first opened in the 1890s), auction rooms, a hospital and a magistrates' court, was the town most often visited by Harefield people. Just before the First World War, the cinema there began to act as a further attraction, a sign that the old introspective self-sufficiency of the village was beginning to break down. Trips further afield were none the less still events to be remembered. As a young man before the First World War, Mr. Statham sometimes went to Watford, and walked the two or so miles from Hill End to Rickmansworth, where he caught a train:

"Sometimes we'd lose the last train, the last train would come home from Watford at 9 o'clock, we'd very often lose that, and then we'd have to walk home from Watford, we didn't use to think anything of

that, dozens of times we've done that, walked back from Watford. There was no lights, we knew our way in the dark really. I tell you another thing what I've done. We did go up to London once or twice, and when we come up we come back and instead of getting out at Denham we went on to Gerrards Cross, and then walked down the railway home at midnight."

People knew each other. 'Everyone was related', and nicknames were common:

"Yes, they all had nicknames. My father was called Corky, that's because we lived in a pub, you see."

There was a full complement of 'characters' who were well known to all:

"There was a very eccentric man, Mr. Turner. And there was another old boy called Pockets and he'd call for him and he'd say "Come on, Pockets, and we'll have a duck race," and he'd get an empty barrel and put it on the pond and they'd put a duck there and the pair of them would get in this barrel in all their clothes and they'd chase this duck round and round, and we used to run like mad, we used to say "Come on, there's a duck race on the pond." And his poor wife she used to stand there with her hands folded like this, and she used to say "Jack you'll drive me mad." That was a great bit of fun."

There was also a somewhat defensive attitude towards outsiders like the canal boatmen:

"The canal was used quite a lot, all these large barges and the horses used to pull the barges along, they used to carry the bricks and all sorts of things when there was the barges. They was always full of something, weren't they? [People] used to live on the barges and when they bought a cottage in Harefield the children came to our school, but we always used to call them the bargee children."

For men at least, much of the time outside working hours was spent in the pubs, most of them small beerhouses like the Spotted Dog:

"They only had one room with benches and wooden tables, and benches in the passage, so in hot weather customers used to sit on the grass verges. Some of their old customers used to go in their living room and play dominoes."

Pubs acted as social centres for all kinds of activity. The larger inns especially contained rooms for Friendly Society and other meetings. In most cases, however, the pub was an informal club for working men, whose influence ran counter to, and possibly deeper than, that of the churches and other 'respectable' organisations. Shops were also important social centres. People carried on conversations across the street, men chatted at the village cross-roads:

'I can remember we used to talk across the village street. We

Facing page: Cleaning the Village Pond, 1913

never moved across the road. We just spoke to one another across the street, gathered together."

Despite the influence of temperance and other organisations, Harefield seems to have been a rather unruly place:

'People got drunk and they had a little fight. They used to say you could have a drink and a fight for twopence."

And again:

"There used to be a fight in the village at the King's Arms nearly every Saturday night. And when there was a fight you couldn't find a policeman anywhere. Old Bugner, he wouldn't have stood up to them [the fighters] five minutes, not them days."

Whether or not because of the disorderly habits of the villagers, a large number of policemen were regularly stationed in Harefield. (There were eight in 1881):

"Oh I knew all the old policemen, there were about twelve or fourteen. Great big fellows they was, you know. I'd meet them in Hill End. One big old fellow, he was supposed to go right down Springwell, he used to say, "Is it all right down there?" I used to say, "Oh yes, all clear". "Oh!" he'd say, "I think I'll toddle off back."

We are perhaps too much inclined to exaggerate the stability, calmness and cohesion of village communities in the past. Poverty, recurrent unemployment and harsh living and working conditions could brutalise people. Between 1878 and 1893 an average of four cases of assault or abuse a year from Harefield were brought before the Uxbridge magistrates, and there was also a stream of indictments for drunk and disorderly conduct. Several of the cases were for assaults on policemen; others were for sexual offences or wife-beating. Other rural communities with large working-class populations seem to have had a similar undercurrent of violence in the 19th and early 20th centuries.

Some of the old communal village activities still survived at the end of the 19th century. Most rural festivals had died out, but the Christmas mummers' play was still performed, and children still went 'garlanding' on May Day in the 1880s, with bunches of flowers tied on to sticks or hoops, singing a traditional song, remembered by Mrs. Breen:

"This brings the merry month of May
The Springtime of the year
We have come to your house
To taste of your strong beer.
If you have got no strong beer
We will be content with small
And take the goodness of your house
And give God thanks for all.

Facing page: The Rose and Crown in 1906

A branch of May we have brought you
And at your door now stand.
It's well spread about and well budded out
By works of our Lord's Hands.
A garland, a garland, a very pretty garland
That ever you wish to see
It's fit for you and fit for me
And fit for the noble Queen."

"They used to open the door and give us a little money, and we said thank you and God bless you all. We used to look forward to that."

This practice seems to have died out at the end of the 19th century. As in many villages, there was a procession of Friendly Societies each Whit Monday, followed by dancing and refreshments; in 1881 according to the *Middlesex Advertiser* the proceedings included tea for 60 working men given by the vicar, who gave a speech on thrift, and listed intemperance, frequent changes of job and the frequent resort to credit as major reasons for poverty. Later the Friendly Society procession was transferred to 'Hospital Sunday' with two bands leading the marchers from the village green to the church. The annual horticultural society shows were also important:

"They used to have two flower shows in the year, one in the hall, what they called the chrysanthemum show, that's all they showed, you see, there. Then they used to have another one in September, a general show, vegetables. My father used to win a lot of prizes."

Many communal activities were held on the green, the true centre of Harefield. Villagers were jealous of their rights over this piece of ground; when the newly-formed Parish Council proposed to put rails round it in 1894, a vociferous group called a parish meeting over the issue, claiming that popular rights were being infringed. Nevertheless, the rails were eventually put up. The green, or 'common' as it was usually called, was the venue for mass celebrations like that in honour of Queen Victoria's Golden Jubilee in 1887, when a dinner was provided for the old people. There was also an annual fair. Tramps regularly dossed down on the common in the summer, spending the winter in the Hillingdon workhouse, and political meetings were held there after the vote was granted to agricultural workers in 1884. These could sometimes be rowdy. When suffragette meetings were arranged by the Stedall family, who rented Harefield Grove from 1908 to 1913, they were disrupted by turfs being thrown at the speakers:

"When we had the suffragettes' meeting, there was old Alf Collett and Snapper Brown, old Sam Filkins, and them, they was going to pull old Mother Stedall and all them in the pond, and the police

Facing page: A Fair on the Common, 1910

couldn't go on the common to stop them. The police could stop them on the highway road, they could stop 'em, see, but when they packed it up, they had to run in Mark's, what is now the King's Arms, out of the way. I think it was old Charlie Brown got the rope, they got a rope all round 'em. Oh yes, that was on the stage. They was going to throw the lot in the pond, and he'd got the rope. . . Oh yes, they actually got away, and then Stedalls moved to Croxley Green then, from the Grove, after that."

The common was also used for sporting events. Harefield was well-known for its football and cricket teams, and visiting teams sometimes came from London:

"Years ago when I was a lad, the bean-feasters used to come down from London with six horses, right from London, and us lads we used to run after them to meet them, and they used to play cricket and football on the common every day, they came to the Cricketers Inn and when they went back, all us lads, we used to run after the coach and what we had to do, we had to turn over heads and heels in the road and then they'd throw us money out. It's true, men from London, you know, from those pubs."

The churches played an important part in the life of the village, but they do not figure very prominently in most people's reminiscences. There were three churches in Harefield, and also a Salvation Army mission which met in the old Malt House for a short period at the end of the 19th century:

"I remember the Salvation Army bringing the War Cry, [the Salvation Army magazine], because my Dad used to say to my mother, "I haven't got enough money for my War Cry". So she used to say "How much do you want?" and he'd say "I want three-halfpence", so she used to give him three-halfpence for his War Cry. He'd say, "I must have a War Cry". He couldn't read, my Father couldn't read or write, but he could reckon money."

Disputes between church and chapel, which seem to have been so important a part of the life of some villages, were notably absent, and people seem to have changed their denominations with equanimity:

"We used to go to the Methodists when we were small because it was near, but when we got bigger we used to go to church every Sunday morning."

Perhaps because neither the Baptists nor the Methodists had resident ministers in Harefield, the Anglicans seem to have had larger congregations, and to have played a bigger part in village life. The vicar, the Reverend Albert Harland, held the living for many years and kept an eye on his flock:

"My grandfather used to take his children, that's my mother and three or four others, down to church every Sunday morning, and

Facing page: Parade of Friendly Societies, 1913

HAREFIELD CHURCH

when he missed, [the vicar] used to come to my granny's and knock at the door, and say "Now, where was Jacob, where was Jacob yesterday? Would he be fighting?" Because he was a fighter. My grandfather was a raw knuckle fighter, yes, up on the common."

Mrs. Dobbs remembered watching the grand families going to church:

"They came from church, they had a high coach with the coachman sitting up with a long whip. I can remember the whip, and we'd all stop then, stand at the side of the road and watch them go by, because we liked to watch the people going to church. Mr. Harland's family all walked to church, behind him or in front of him — he was a ponderous old chap. She was a little lady."

Children first came into contact with the church or chapels through the Sunday Schools:

"[We] didn't go to church very much, but we were obliged to go to Sunday School."

The churches are remembered for the bounty they distributed, and for their welfare activities, as well as for their spiritual aspect. The Nonconformists were vigorous in promoting weekday functions which would lure people away from the pubs. The Memorial Hall, used by the Wesleyans, was an important centre of village life, used for temperance meetings, evening lectures, and for what would now be called adult literacy classes. The Wesleyans also organised 'tea meetings":

"All the gentry in Harefield they used to have a table there, you see, then get these teas where you bought your tickets outside, then you could choose which table you'd like to sit at. It was a missionary tea and all the money used to go to the missionaries, it used to be packed full, it used to be beautiful, once a year."

The leading inhabitants of the village figured prominently in church life and also promoted social activities in their own right. As a three- or four-year-old, Mr. Harman remembered being invited to treats at Breakspears, Harefield Grove, Harefield Park and the Vicarage. From the 1890s until his death in 1921, Alfred Henry Tarleton of Breakspears performed some of the functions of 'squire' of the village, founding the Breakspear Institute in 1896, and playing a leading part in the parish council. The Institute, built no doubt with the intention of providing a counter-attraction to the pubs, offered facilities for reading and games, and ran successful football and cricket teams. Social activities were also put on at the asbestos works. The manager, Mr. McCallum, lived in a house by the factory which was called, significantly though incorrectly, the Manor House. He was an organiser of the local Conservatives and a prominent figure on the

Facing page Top: Visitors to Harefield outside The Cricketers, 1911
Facing page Bottom: Harefield Church, 1908

parish council. Yet, despite these paternalistic efforts, the reminiscences of working people make one doubt how deeply they were influenced by the ideas of their 'betters'. Their social life grew naturally out of poverty and hard work, and these experiences could only make the rich appear as outsiders, however benevolent they were. It was only when incomes began to rise significantly, between the wars, that the barriers imposed by poverty began to crumble; and then people soon discovered that the old self-sufficient life of the community had begun to disappear too.

POSTSCRIPT

Harefield has undergone many drastic changes within living memory. Once a place in which most people both lived and worked, it is now, like most villages near London, a predominantly dormitory community. And like many other villages it has undergone something like a social revolution. Eighty years ago there was a powerful landowning squirearchy and a very large working class made up mainly of unskilled labourers. Today the old leaders of village society have disappeared, there is a large middle class, and the material conditions of life for the working people have changed out of all recognition. Many of the present inhabitants have moved into Harefield since the Second World War, and expansion still continues. In all these respects Harefield can be said to have mirrored many of the changes that have taken place in Britain as a whole during the 20th century.

Debate still rages, and probably always will, about whether these changes have been for the better. Have the material gains been bought at too high a price? On this question the memories of old people can throw an interesting but rather ambiguous light. There is general agreement that in places like Harefield, widespread poverty bred a sense of community which has largely disappeared. Another common assertion is that although people were poorer than they are today, their needs were fewer and more easily satisfied. Certainly the reminiscences of Harefield give little indication of widespread anger or frustration at poor living conditions: 'We just didn't take any notice, it was just as it is today, it seemed the usual thing.' On the other hand, it is only too easy for us to distort or romanticise the conditions of the past; we are sometimes so conscious of the defects of our own way of life that we wilfully conjure up some mythical 'golden age' in which life was simpler and more satisfying.

We are perhaps especially inclined to idealise the past when we look at the English countryside. Yet an over-idealised picture of rural life will not bear close examination. Rural England was a complex mixture of good and bad, like the England of today. Few people would willingly choose to go back to the material conditions of life and work experienced by many of the working people of early

20th-century Harefield, however much they might be attracted by the simpler life, and the sense of 'belonging' which undoubtedly existed. The gradual alleviation of poverty in the lifetimes of the people whose memories are preserved in these pages has ushered in new problems, but these problems will not be solved by constructing a false picture of the past. By trying to understand what the past was really like from people who experienced it themselves, we may find it easier to understand the forces which have shaped our own way of life.

LIST OF SOURCES

Reminiscences of: Mrs. Breen; Mr. Blower; Mr. Brooker; The Misses Coster; Mr. and Mrs. Dobbs; Mr. and Mrs. Gough; Mrs. Green; Mr. Hale; Mr. Harman; Mrs. Kempster; Mr. Lofty; Mr. Marsden; Mr. Marshall; Mr. Statham; Mrs. Thomas; Mr. Tilly; Mrs. Westbrook; Mrs. Winship.
(Edited transcripts of most of these tapes are in Harefield Public Library).

Public Record Office:
Census returns for 1881 (RG11/1332)
Agricultural returns for 1880 (MAF 68/706)

Parliamentary Papers:
1865 vol. xxvi. pp. 230-1. (Report on Rural Housing).

Middlesex Advertiser, in Uxbridge Public Library, articles relating to Harefield, transcribed by Mrs. Margaret Evans.
Harefield W.E.A. Local History Group, *Harefield at that Time of Day* (1978). This work contains several suggestions for further reading.
W. Goatman, *Harefield and Her Church* (2nd edn. 1972).
Victoria County History of Middlesex, vol. iii.
Kelly's Directory of Middlesex, (1899 and other edns).
King's Directory of Uxbridge (various dates).